Outrageously Fulfilling Relationships

An Outrageous Guide to Creating Uncommonly Blissful Partnerships

(hint- it's an inside job)

Randy Ferguson, MA

Heart Centered Communications, Inc., Publisher

Outrageously Fulfilling Relationships

An Outrageous Guide to Creating
Uncommonly Blissful Partnerships
By Randy Ferguson, MA

Published by:
Heart Centered Communications, Inc.
7101 W Yale Ave Suite 3603
Denver, CO 80227-3576 U.S.A.
www.LCAProject.com

Copyright © 2006 by Randy Ferguson

Library of Congress Control Number: 2005932338

Ferguson, Randy
Outrageously fulfilling relationships: an outrageous guide to creating
uncommonly blissful partnerships / Randy Ferguson. – 1stnd ed.
P. cm.

ISBN 0-9772758-0-9 (pb.)
9780977275809 (pb.)

Printed in the United States of America

To that wonderful indescribable
Something in the Universe who
gives us what we need
before we know to ask

To my precious family
who has always been there for me,
even when I was a kid and
flushed the sheets down the toilet

And especially
to you

"Master your ability to create the experience of loving,
and you will have already won the game of life.
Without internal access to love, no person or quantity of
possessions will ever come close to filling the emptiness.
Discover your natural ability to generate love and
two magical events are inevitable.
First, you will reveal your true identity, which is love itself.
Second, you will savor a level of bliss rarely
demonstrated in the world."

- Randy Ferguson

Acknowledgements

Like many of you, I have had the best parents in the whole world. Dad taught me responsibility and logic. He taught me how things work. Mom taught me love.

My brother, Bill, has been one of my most significant mentors. So much of what is shared in these pages, flows from his keen insight. Janice, my sister, is a beacon of love in the world. She has taught me patience and faith.

My daughter Heather has taught me the power of forgiveness, especially for myself, and the tenacious beauty that blossoms over time in a father-daughter relationship.

I thank the thousands of sacred beings who have attended my seminars. Their questions, their struggles, their very presence, have challenged me to grow. It has been such an honor to spend time with them.

To Amy and Jenny, former wives one and two, respectively and respectfully, thank you for teaching me to reach deeply inside myself to discover my responsibility. Thank you for showing me that no love, no matter how magnificent, is immune to the laws of relationship.

Steven Vannoy, you are the mentor's mentor. Thank you for showing me how a teacher can walk his talk and live from the heart. Craig Ross thank you for showing me how a student can slingshot past his teacher, leaving amazing good in his wake.

Werner Erhard, the incredible staff and students at the University of Santa Monica, the team at Pathways to Leadership - you all have been phenomenally instrumental in my personal evolution. How can I sufficiently express my gratitude for something as priceless as awareness?

Dave Robison and Jan Ratcliffe (graphics artists extraordinaire), thank you. Christine Hubbard, I so appreciate your remarkable photography skills. Cindy Montoya, Sandy Forte, Melodie Matice, Doug Barnes, Karol Barton, Janet Gunn, and Donna Morgan - thank you for taking the time to share your extra ordinary insight, editing and creativity. You are all gifts in my life.

Dear Gail, thank you for showing me that the past does not equal the future. Thank you for being my best friend and especially for bringing Katie into my life. In partnership with you, I am discovering something I've never known before; the bliss available in family.

There is nothing I have to give that has not first been given to me. Nothing. So my ultimate expression of thanks goes to the Divine Spirit who saw fit to grace me with this awesome gift of life and the consciousness to appreciate it.

Table of Contents

WHY BAD RELATIONSHIPS HAPPEN TO GOOD PEOPLE

Why don't relationships work like an old Disney movie? Boy meets girl. They fall in love. Get married. Make babies. Actually speak to each other at dinner. What happened to growing old and happy together, 'till death do us part?

I don't remember asking for arguments, hurt feelings, and the silent treatment. When did I order things like loneliness, jealousy and divorce? I mean, what did I do to deserve all this? Is there a way of looking at relationships that makes any kind of sense...or does God just have a masochistic sense of humor?

Not too long ago, the average Joe thought the world was flat. As you might imagine, this made any long distance navigation difficult, confusing, and falling off the edge was more than a little frightening. Then some fool proposed the outrageous notion that the earth was round. Eventually, the idea caught on which made possible, logical navigation and Caribbean cruises.

So here are some other outrageous notions...basic principles...that might start to answer some of those "why me?" Questions:

Basic Principle #1: Earth is a school. The purpose of this school is to teach us the lessons we need to mature as human beings. (Specifically, to learn how to live congruently with our basic nature which is one of love.)

Basic Principle #2: We are all students, and school is now in session...in fact, it's always in session.

Basic Principle #3: Principles #1 and #2 are true whether we like it or not.

Basic Principle #4: This means we are brought just the right relationships and circumstances in our lives, to teach us our daily lessons. When we focus attention on ourselves...to see where we are personally responsible and make appropriate course corrections... we learn and grow. When we choose to ignore the lesson, to focus on who's to blame and how life's unfair...we discover Basic Principle #5.

Basic Principle #5: Our school is caring enough to bring us the lesson over and over and over again, until we're ready to listen. Does this sound heartless? It is not. Life is committed to showing us a better way, a way of profound fulfillment. Every day we are given opportunities to learn, to forgive, to clean up our mistakes, to express our caring, to go for our dreams.

Basic Principle #6: What makes our lives so difficult is that most of us are totally committed to our comfort, whether or not it's fulfilling. The earth school, however, is totally committed to our fulfillment, whether or not it's comfortable (have you noticed?). When we live our lives contrary to the school curriculum, we create tremendous stress for ourselves, and life can feel like swimming up a waterfall.

Basic Principle #7: Who you are, is incredibly precious. So precious that the universe has been set up to educate you. Please consider the possibility that everything you can perceive (even that which you call terrible) is a gift dedicated to the evolution of your wisdom, and there truly is no such thing as mere coincidence.

When you think about it, holding relationships in this context, opens a remarkable opportunity. Is it possible that as we grow personally in both our wisdom and skills, we can develop a level of mastery in how we relate to others? As we demonstrate this mastery with others, is it possible that people will relate back to us in a way that reflects more joy and satisfaction? Is it possible that creating outrageously fulfilling relationships truly is an inside job?

Here is a promise I solemnly offer to you. As you practice the principles described in this little book, the quality of both your relationships and your life will be significantly enhanced.

Just imagine. It's one year from today. You have been diligent in learning the lessons of this earth school. You have put your insights to work and now see life from a higher altitude. Your relationships both romantic and otherwise, are a continual source of tremendous joy. What does it feel like to have literally manifested the dreams of your heart in this arena?

SELF-LOVING...NO LONGER
JUST A LUXURY

What would you do in the following scenario?

You're walking through town and hear the desperate cries of a child. Turning around, you witness an act of cruelty; a parent is striking his/her little one, with a belt...over and over again. Every time the child tries to stand, the parent unleashes another flurry of abuse, unceasingly, without mercy.

How would you handle this situation? Would you be incensed enough to take some kind of action? I suspect most of us would.

Yet, there is a similar form of brutality taking place right in our midst on a daily basis, that is no less vicious, yet usually goes ignored. I am referring, of course, to the way we treat ourselves.

In our culture, we're not taught that we have a relationship with our 'self.' We learn about managing relationships with our parents, family, significant other and friends, but not with the one person who is always, always, always there with us.

Through unknowing neglect, that relationship with self for so many people, has become nothing less than abusive. All too often, we have treated ourselves like the child, beaten by the parent; and we have failed to take action. We've forgotten that in each one of us, lives a sacred spirit, no less precious than that little one.

This abuse isn't necessarily physical; it can take many forms. For example, do you ever...

• Harshly judge yourself?
• Speak to others in a way that invokes alienation or retaliation?
• Make agreements that are impossible to uphold?
• Say 'yes' when you mean to say 'no' and vice versa?
• Feel chronically trapped in circumstances beyond your control?
• Put yourself last, avoiding the very action that would nurture you?
• Push away the very love for which your heart yearns?

The cumulative impact of this self-disregard, takes the wind of life, right out of our sails. We end up destroying the nurturing required for healthy self-esteem. And isn't it our foundation of self-esteem upon which we build success or failure in relationships and in life?

My brother shared something a while back that got my attention. He said, "You know, Randy, the world doesn't need changing. "I told him he was nuts, and asked him to explain. He said, "If we changed the planet, if we ended starvation and crime and tyranny and pollution...and yet there was no love, in a matter of days, all the atrocities would be right back."

He said, "What the world needs so desperately, is to learn how to love. Only then, can the world change in a way that makes a difference."

It seems to me that learning to love like this, has to begin with us individually. So here's the question: What will it take to create a significant shift in our ability to experience self-loving?

We can begin by recognizing that we do, indeed, have a relationship with our self. We can deliberately treat our self with the same caring and compassion we would offer an innocent child. Speak to that little one inside ourselves with tenderness. When times get tough, pour on the unconditional acceptance. Accept and appreciate the beauty in who we have become, just the way we are.

When self-loving becomes a habit in our lives, rather than a luxury, we will relate to life in a way that works. Then get ready for outrageously fulfilling relationships, because we will know in our hearts, we are worthy of them.

EIGHT RELATIONSHIP MYTHS THAT LEAD TO DISASTER

What's it like coming home to a war zone? Arguing. Anger. The silent treatment. Home, where marital bliss degenerates to combat for couples. How can something that started out so wonderful, turn so bitter? I mean, what's wrong with this picture?

Before you call the Terminator, attorney at law, you might consider this: In our culture, we're taught certain rules about relating. AND MANY OF THESE RULES ACTUALLY DESTROY RELATIONSHIPS! It's like driving in Boston with a map of Albuquerque. Lots of dead ends. Lots of frustration. When you think about it, we learned most of our relationship skills from two primary sources; our parents and television. For many of us, that's a very scary thought.

So let's flush out a few of these myths. You might want to take a moment and ask yourself if you've been unconsciously following some of these guides to disaster. You might call them, "Eight Keys to Outrageously Painful Relationships."

Key #1: IF I'M IN A PAINFUL RELATIONSHIP, IT'S OBVIOUSLY BECAUSE THE OTHER PERSON HAS A PROBLEM; IT'S CERTAINLY NOT ME. (This rule is great for giving away your personal power. As long as you're focusing on the other person, guess who doesn't have to take responsibility for constructive action?)

Key #2: THE BEST WAY TO HANDLE MY HURT IS TO IGNORE IT. I'LL JUST STUFF IT WHEN IT COMES UP. IT'S SURE TO PASS. (Pass right into your stomach, or maybe your heart. What toll do you suppose this takes on our bodies after a decade or three?)

Key #3: EVERYBODY KNOWS THE SOURCE OF LOVE AND CARING IS ANOTHER PERSON. (This may be outright heresy, but I thought that my feelings lived inside me. What's that other person doing with MY feelings? Give 'em back!)

Key #4: A TRULY GREAT RELATIONSHIP HAS NO CONFLICT. (Did you ever wonder what happened AFTER they rode off into the sunset? Growth perhaps?)

Key #5: IF I REALLY APPLY MYSELF, I KNOW I CAN MOLD MY PARTNER INTO A WORTHWHILE PERSON. (God will be so relieved to know He can take a little break, having found such a capable replacement.)

Key#6: I CAN HIDE THE TRUTH FROM MY SPOUSE, FROM MY CHILDREN AND THE PEOPLE AROUND ME. THEY'LL NEVER KNOW. (Right, and the Emperor has a great new wardrobe.)

Key #7: THE MORE I HANG ON TO THE PERSON I LOVE, THE LESS THEY'LL WANT TO LEAVE ME. (This makes sense. Remember how attracted you were to someone who tried to suffocate you with their clingingness.)

Key #8: I REALLY SHOULD BE ABLE TO FIGURE OUT THIS RELATIONSHIP STUFF ALL BY MYSELF (And once you've accomplished that, perhaps you'll try your own neurosurgery.)

Have you heard the latest definition of insanity? It's doing the same thing, over and over again, and expecting a different result. If our relationships haven't been working, and we truly want positive change, doesn't it make sense that we might have to operate differently?

So here's a challenge for you. Take a couple of minutes for yourself, contemplate each of these 8 points and answer these two questions: How can you turn around each of these myths into a constructive principle? How can you transform disaster into the quality of relationships your heart so yearns for?

HEALING AFTER THEY SAY GOODBYE

"I'm leaving you. I just don't love you anymore. Good bye."

I don't know about you, but for me, these are some of the most painful words I've ever heard. For most people, breaking up is hard to do, especially when the other person does the leaving. It hurts, and it hurts deeply. Self-esteem shrivels to nothing, revealing an emptiness that can last for years.

How can someone heal a heartache that big? Is it even possible? The answer is yes. Absolutely, yes. When you are ready to heal, there is a way that works. You do not have to live in that ongoing emotional pain, unless you choose to. You can regain that feeling of self-love and confidence without jumping right back into the next dysfunctional relationship. The first step is to understand the principle of attachment.

In our culture, we are taught "You ain't nobody 'till somebody loves you." We're taught that the source of love comes from another person. We're taught that when they leave, love leaves. So we try to hang on to our partner to avoid losing love. In our hanging on, we become attached to them. Our well being then becomes totally dependent upon our partner behaving in a certain way, namely, sticking around. To be attached is to give away all our power to create love, to someone else. In attachment we set the stage for our own emotional carnage.

The key to releasing attachment is to truly in our heart, let the person go. Often we're afraid to let go. We're afraid that if we let go, they'll leave. If that's the case with you, you might want to notice that your hanging on doesn't keep them around anyway. In fact, the more you're attached to someone, the more you drive the person away. Remember how you felt when someone tried clinging on to you? Yet many people remain emotionally attached, even long after their partner has moved on.

Here are four steps to letting go of attachment, regaining your dignity, and getting on with the business of joyful living:

Step 1) Notice that the idea of losing this person is upsetting. Admit that you are attached. Once you tell the truth, the healing can begin.

Step 2) Create a willingness to let them go. In your heart, give them total permission to be gone from your life, forever.

Step 3) At this point, you might feel a sadness. Know that this feeling is coming up to be healed. Let the sadness come. Don't fight it. Let the tears come if you can. Be like the child who cries fully without reservation, and then goes out to play.

Step 4) Fill the emptiness by building a relationship with the one human being who has never left your side, you. Begin nurturing a joyful relationship with yourself. Discover the key of bringing your joy to a relationship, rather than trying to squeeze joy from a relationship.

When you truly let go of your attachment, then look back on the whole process, you will see that you have grown tremendously as a person. As you grow personally, you begin to attract better life partners. You may even find yourself saying, "Thank you, God, for getting me out of a relationship where I wasn't appreciated."

WHY SHOULD I FORGIVE?

Have you ever been in an abusive relationship? With a boss, a mate, or perhaps a family member? Have you ever been betrayed... filled with bitterness, toward someone you used to call "friend?"

People say we should forgive, but in most cases, they weren't there to witness the hurting. They say we should forgive and forget, then get on with our lives. Most of us agree with, getting on with our lives. We say "maybe" to forgetting...but why in the world should we forgive?

For you. Forgive them for your own well being.

If you think about it, resentment lives in the heart of the person doing the resenting. The person you direct your resentment toward, is probably off in Vail skiing, having a wonderful time...and you're stuck back here with the resentment.

People don't realize the price they pay in harboring a resentment. Resentment is incredibly expensive! It costs you your joy, your peace, your ability to focus. It fills you with thoughts contrary to your own integrity. Even if you're in a great new relationship, it's only a matter of time before that old resentment shows up in one form or another with your new partner. It's like going out to the dumpster, retrieving decaying garbage and setting it on the dining room table. Yuck!

Resentment is a parasite that feeds on the human heart. If you feed it long enough, it will consume you...first emotionally, then physically. Personally, I think we are far too precious to treat ourselves this way.

There are several reasons why we are reluctant to forgive. Often, people carry resentment in order to make a point. The assumption here is, if you resent someone enough, that person is eventually going to straighten right up and behave just the way you think they should. Don't hold your breath for this one.

Another reason we resent is that we think forgiveness would in some way, condone the perpetrator's actions. It would be saying that what they did to us was "OK." Please know that forgiveness is not at all about approving their inappropriate behavior! Forgiveness is about our own healing. It's about setting ourselves free inside.

Is forgiveness about being a doormat? Absolutely not! It takes courage to move forward in life...to maintain our personal boundaries...to say "no" when we need to...and to do it with an open heart. When you're ready...here are some keys to forgiveness:

- Creating willingness is a choice you freely make in your own heart. If you are not willing to forgive, that's OK...but the consequence is, you get to keep the resentment, and everything that goes with it. The willingness to do...creates the ability to do. Until you're willing, nothing changes.

- Be willing to fully experience all the hurt that comes up. Underneath the anger, is the hurt. Don't resist the hurt. Embrace it. Cry if you can. Release all the sadness and let it go.

- Notice that, just like you, they did the best they could with a very limited awareness. If they were wiser and more aware, they would have done things very differently, but they weren't.

- Then forgive yourself. Forgive yourself for anything you've done in retaliation. Forgive yourself for attracting a dysfunctional relationship. Forgive yourself for making the mistakes that destroyed the experience of loving, and give yourself permission to be who you are, a precious human being with limitations.

ELIMINATING OVERWHELM...
RECLAIMING YOUR PERSONAL DIGNITY

What does it feel like to be overwhelmed? Your employer decides to downsize. Then your rent check bounces. Little Suzy gets the chicken pox. And the new puppy eats your prize tulips. And the laundry looks like a tourist attraction. And your spouse won't talk. And...

Overwhelm is that sense of hopelessness we feel when life's circumstances appear bigger than we are. In time, this state of overwhelm can lead to depression and severe health problems. It's no fun. It prevents us from being truly present in relationships, and creates a tendency to blame the people we love. Overwhelm just plain hurts.

Want to trade in your overwhelm for some joyful relief? Here's how:

Recognize that the circumstances in our lives do NOT cause overwhelm. What causes overwhelm, is how we relate to our circumstances. Does this seem far-fetched? I have proof! Read on.

We relate to our lives in one of two ways; either we are living in "pro-action" or we are living "in reaction."

Living in reaction is living the life of a victim. Life is doing it to me. The circumstances are bigger than I am. I am just a helpless leaf in the rapids. What I think, what I do, and who I am, does not really make an impact.

Living in pro-action is stepping into the opportunity of being alive. No circumstance has the power to determine my attitude. I am responsible for the outcome of my life. It is my honor and my duty to create a life that works.

Make a choice. From moment to moment we get to choose. We either live in reaction or we live in pro-action. To live in reaction is to choose death. To live in pro-action is to choose life. We make this choice consciously or unconsciously. And not choosing, is not an option.

If our choice is to live in pro-action, the next step is to take a quick inventory of the challenges in our lives. Notice that those challenges are there, whether we like them or not. Notice that not liking our circumstances doesn't change a thing. Give up the notion that life should be easy. Come face to face with the realization that these challenges are not just going to handle themselves.

Generate in your heart, the commitment and the conviction to do whatever it takes to handle the circumstances in your life. Get psyched, and step up to the plate. If the mess in your life is big, create a commitment that is bigger. If you're 90% committed, your task will be very difficult. If you're 100% committed, your task will be relatively easy. Generate in your heart that 100% commitment, and get ready to kick some butt.

Take action. Reclaim your time. Go after the 9 foot monster and tell the 8 1/2 foot monster it will just have to wait. Savor the victory of handling what has been handling you.

And here's the proof. Notice that the instant you generate that 100% commitment to do whatever it takes, the overwhelm evaporates into thin air. And this is true even before a single unworkability in your life has changed!

Remember the words of Yogi Bashan, "Suffering is what takes place between the moment you know what you need to do...and the moment you commit to doing it." And wasn't it Thoreau who said, "It's what we're NOT doing that exhausts us."

FEAR OF DATING

A while back I realized that if I was ever going to find a lifemate, I would have to become proactive in the process...you know...actually DO something. Frankly, the very thought of dating again terrified me. Yet, I didn't want to spend the rest of my life alone, watching movies of other people having fun. So, how could I overcome my fear, and go about meeting new prospects?

If you think about it, whenever we're afraid, there's something we don't want to experience. In this case, it's probably rejection. And here's a key: The greater our resistance to experiencing something, the greater our fear. This means we actually create fear, in our unwillingness to feel a certain way. Conversely, the more we are willing to experience something, the less our fear of it.

Am I suggesting that we create a willingness to be rejected? Absolutely! Be totally willing to experience rejection over and over again. Does this sound masochistic? It's not. In our actions, set up life to succeed. Anticipate success. But in our hearts, be totally willing to be rejected. When we are truly willing to experience the worst, our fear takes a hike, and we can start having some fun. What a concept! How might this look in real life?

Scenario #1: You're at a party. There, across the room, is someone you would really like to meet. As you move a little closer, guess what comes up? Fear!

"What if I say something stupid? What if they think I'm a jerk? What if I spill my bean dip?"

On second thought, you decide to flip through a magazine. No risk. No results.

Scenario #2: You're at a party. There, across the room, is someone you would really like to meet. Those same fear-based reasons to quit, stampede through your head. But this time you are aware of the process.

"Yes, maybe I'll fumble my words. Maybe they'll think I'm a nerd. And there's life after spilled bean dip!"

You create the willingness to fail, then move forward anyway. Remember, feeling fear doesn't necessarily mean stop.

Scenario #1 is about backing down from the directives of our heart. As a way of life, this philosophy will cost us our confidence, our vitality, and what we truly desire. Scenario #2 is about stepping into the promise of life. It's about going for it. It's about expanding our personal power, our dignity, and our joy.

So whether we like it or not, we get to choose. Do we wait for fear to leave before we move forward? Or do we feel the fear, and go for our dreams?

Personally, I'm going for the gusto. See you at the party!

ARE YOU WEARING MATE REPELLENT?

I was lonely. I knew that if I could just find the right sweetheart, out there in Singleland, everything would turn out fine. Decked out with some new clothes, I went a-hunting.

There she is! My lifemate. Yes, I could spend the rest of my life with her. The woman who will bear my children. I ask her to dance. She offers me that kind of half-smile especially reserved for social lepers, and says maybe later. Right. Christmas, perhaps.

Undaunted, driven by hormones and some kind of love vacuum, I forge on. The next three attempts meet with similar rebuffs. And it's off to the rest room to regroup. Poised in front of the mirror, I review my check list:

Hair combed?...Check.

Shirt tucked?...Check.

No foreign objects hanging from my nose?...Check.
Ah-ha! Now I see the problem. It's those big red letters stamped on my forehead, "Caution, Ladies: The surgeon general has determined that this male specimen is in desperate need of companionship.

Any form of kindness shown, may result in being emotionally smothered, and will most certainly be hazardous to your emotional health."

So what's going on here? The greater my need for a partner, the less I'm likely to find one? Don't tell me dating is like borrowing money; you only get the loan if you can prove you don't need it. I mean, what's the deal here? Is this some kind of sick cosmic humor?

No. It's just the universe reminding me that I have to find love in my own heart, before I can find it in another. The instant I attribute my joy and wholeness to another human being, I create a dependency on that person. The recipient of this dependency usually feels clinged to...smothered. And most people don't like to be smothered. Most people hate it. Conclusion? Desperately needing companionship, is the world's most effective form of mate repellent.

That deep yearning for another, that intense loneliness, is indeed a warning sign that something is missing from life. But what's missing doesn't come packaged in a mini-skirt or three piece suit. What's missing is self-love. What's missing is a deep experience of self-acceptance and self-appreciation.

When we can create in our hearts the genuine willingness to be alone, and to be alone forever, what we are left with is our relationship with self. So how do you want to relate to you?

Consider the possibility that when we bring our joy

to a relationship, instead of trying to get joy from a relationship, the desperate urgency for another falls away. We start to have fun again. And of course, that makes us incredibly attractive.

MANAGING YOUR MENTAL MONSTERS

You start a car trip in a great mood, which eventually degenerates into a heated argument. Finally, you arrive at your destination feeling lousy. And then have an enormous insight. You realize...you were the only one in the car!

We all have an inner conversation that has a profound effect on our lives. It determines how we feel about ourselves, others and life. It is the ongoing language that perpetuates our day to day reality, the command voice that influences how we relate to every situation.

When this voice goes unmanaged, it can often become harshly self-critical, sometimes downright abusive. Like a chain saw gnawing at our self-esteem, the unmanaged mind can create tremendous damage, and become a source of great suffering. And this is true whether we are aware of the voice or not.

Our inner conversation also has a tendency to become a self-fulfilling prophesy. I know a woman who, in her childhood, was deeply hurt by her father. As she matured, her inner voice constantly reminded her that all men were dangerous and couldn't be trusted. To protect herself, she acted cold and distant whenever a man got too close. In reaction to her distancing, men would back away, which of course provided more evidence that men were dangerous and couldn't be trusted.

Until she is willing to heal her own inner conversation about men, the pattern will most likely repeat indefinitely.

So sometimes it is helpful to stand back and just listen to the voice. Listen to the conversation in your mind and the words that come out of your mouth. Imagine that you are a powerful computer, and your inner conversation is the programming that will determine your entire future.

The rule of thumb here, is to let go of any self-sabotaging speaking or thinking, unless that's the way you want it to be. As Emerson said, "The ancestor of every action is a thought."

To manage your inner conversation, just be still and listen. Notice what you're thinking. Notice that your thoughts are like a river. They come and they go. You may not be able to stop the river, but you do get to choose the thoughts you pull out of it. If your inner voice isn't supporting you, just let the thoughts float downstream. Then deliberately generate a conversation that truly furthers you.

How we manage our thinking, is probably the single greatest factor in what maintains or destroys our experience of love in relationships. The more we focus and dwell on our partner's faults, the more we destroy the dynamic of unconditional acceptance and deep appreciation. The more we focus and dwell on their strengths and qualities, the more powerful our love for them becomes.

There's a story of a young Indian brave who once experienced a kind of mental anguish. He went to his chief and said he felt like there were two dogs fighting in his head; a good dog and a bad dog. In his turmoil, he asked the chief which dog would eventually win. The chief replied, "My son, the dog that wins, will be the dog that you feed."

THE GIFT IN UPSETS

When I'm really upset about something, there's usually a period of time when the last thing I want is good advice. Leave me alone! I'll just keep my upset for a while!...thank you very much!

Upsets happen in the best of relationships. However, if the upset continues over a long period of time, it can destroy the experience of love. And the absence of love, over time, is a formula for separation. So, when the suffering gets big enough, I may actually want to do something radical, like heal the upset.

Important Point: To have outrageously fulfilling relationships, give up the expectation that upsets should never occur...and discover how to MOVE THROUGH the upset, as fast as possible. If you have a persistent upset in your life, and are ready for a little inner peace and clarity, the following steps may be of value:

STEP 1: NOTICE THAT YOU ARE UPSET. Slamming doors. Raging in traffic. Asking for divorce. Notice those subtle little indicators that something's not quite right. Admit the truth..."I'm upset!"

STEP 2: CREATE THE WILLINGNESS AND THE COMMITMENT TO HEAL THE UPSET. You're in charge here. Nothing changes unless you say so. You have the option of hanging on to an upset for years or releasing it quickly. If you choose freedom from upset, begin with the conviction to do what it takes.

STEP 3: SEPARATE YOUR UPSET FROM THE SITUATION. Imagine your upset as a giant watermelon. Imagine taking a Samurai sword and slicing that watermelon right in half. (Note: it's the upset we're slicing in half, not the other person). One half of that watermelon is the circumstances in your life and the other half is how you are reacting to the circumstances. These are two totally separate things. Then place 100% of our attention on the half called "how you are reacting to the circumstances." Why? Because upset doesn't live in the circumstances. Upset lives in you.

STEP 4: NOTICE THAT YOU ARE RESISTING THE WAY THINGS ARE. The source of suffering is resistance. If you are upset, ask yourself, "What is it specifically that I am resisting?" Acknowledge that in each moment, life is a certain way. When you resist the way life is, you get upset. You lose your peace and your clarity.

STEP 5: GIVE UP YOUR DEMAND THAT LIFE BE DIFFERENT THAN THE WAY THAT IT IS. In each moment, isn't life exactly the way that it is? Aren't the people in your life exactly the way that they are? And aren't you exactly the way that you are? And isn't this true whether you like it or not? Let go of demanding the impossible and accept life the way that it is.

STEP 6: EXPERIENCE ANY HURT THAT MIGHT COME UP. When you truly let go of unrealistic expectations, you may notice a sadness come up. Let it come. It's resisting your hurt that keeps it stuck. Feel the sadness. Cry if you can. Let the hurt come and go, just like those little masters we call children.

STEP 7: ACCEPT AND APPRECIATE THE WAY THINGS ARE. Notice the experience of peace is a direct function of our capacity to accept. Appreciate your life and the people in it. Appreciate yourself... just the way you are.

STEP 8: TAKE WHATEVER ACTION YOU NEED TO TAKE. From this place of serenity, we can see clearly. Now is the time to focus on the other half of the watermelon; the circumstances around the upset. Take whatever high-integrity action is needed to move forward.

Each time we use upset for our growing, we gain strength and wisdom. Remember the words of Mother Theresa, "I know God will not give me anything I can't handle. Sometimes I just wish that He didn't trust me so much."

THE POWER OF POSITIVE ANGER

Anger has got to win first place for the most misunderstood, most misused emotion. In our failure to understand anger, we have created tremendous suffering, and lost a powerful source of personal energy.

In loving relationships, many of us operate under the assumption that there is no place for anger towards our partner. Over time, this can create a real problem because at some point, we ARE going to get angry with our special someone. But if there's no permission to express our upset, our tendency is to suppress it. Then it festers and grows like an untreated infection. No fun!!

Let's begin by dispelling some age-old illusions about anger. First of all, anger itself...is not bad. This notion may be hard to accept at first, given some of our painful histories. So it might be useful to view anger as just a form of energy...an energy that can be expressed constructively or destructively. Most of us are very familiar with destructive expressions of anger. Yelling. Screaming. Breaking things. Breaking people.

If anger was expressed destructively in our child-hoods, we may have sworn passionately to never be like that. We may have decided that anger was a terrible thing, to be avoided at all costs. What we didn't notice is, whether we like it or not, we're human beings...and human beings get angry.

So how can anger possibly be used for good? Have you ever put off accomplishing an important task, then become so angry, you created the energy to complete the job? Perhaps it was cleaning the garage, or working out, or standing up for yourself. How did you feel afterwards? What you experienced, was tapping into the constructive energy of anger. Used positively, anger can be a furnace of personal power.

Another anger illusion is the assumption that unexpressed anger just goes away. But the truth is, if our anger isn't expressed outwardly, it gets expressed inwardly. It gets expressed destructive-ly against ourselves. How do you know if you're carrying self-directed anger? Do any of these symp-toms sound familiar: Impatience? Harsh judgment of others? Chronic stress? Over-reacting? Depression?

Here are some keys that have profoundly improved my own relationship with anger:

• Know that it's OK to be angry! It's not a place we want to live for any length of time, but its occa-sional presence is part of being human. When you can truly accept your anger, you will feel an inner freedom, a restoration of your personal power and a new sense of dignity. In fact you can even have fun with it (Arrrrrgg!!!...I'm SOOOO MAD right now!!!) And then move into a place of hysterical laughter.

- Being angry doesn't mean someone has to get hurt, physically or emotionally. Don't take your anger out on another...or on yourself. Remember, you always pay a price for destructive anger.

- Express your anger constructively. Don't hold it in. Express your anger in a way that supports you. Go work out. Write in your journal. Yell in your car. Beat your rugs. Mow your yard.

- In relationships, mutually agree to allow the constructive expression of anger. Share how you feel without blaming your partner.

- Remember, anything we're not willing to experience runs our life. The more we're willing to experience our anger, the less it gets to run us.

Arrrrrgggg!

EMPOWERMENT...HOW TO CREATE ECSTASY IN RELATIONSHIPS

Love is what makes the difference in relationships. When the experience of love is present, relationships thrive...and when it's absent, relationships die. In fact, aren't those moments of loving, what really determine our very quality of life? Emmet Fox writes, "If only you could love enough, you would be the happiest and most powerful being in the world."

As a culture, however, we know almost nothing about love. We operate under the assumption that love is optional. It isn't. Could this be why over half our marriages end in divorce? In my seminars, I ask people, "How many of you love to be loved?" All hands are raised. Then I ask, "What is love and how does it work?". Nary a hand in sight. As a thirteen year old participant once exclaimed, "Here's this thing called love...it's the most important thing in the whole world...and nobody knows what it is!" From the mouths of babes...

But what if there was something we could do, as simple as turning on a light switch, that could turn on love? How would our relationships be different if we had the power to create love at will? The vital key to creating more love in our lives, the single most important dynamic in any healthy relationship, is the principle of empowerment.

Empowerment is giving the gift of authentic, unconditional acceptance and deep appreciation. It is not flattery, which demands something in return. Empowerment is seeing the real beauty in another, and letting them know from your heart. Just watch people's eyes light up when you empower them for a job well done. Or thank them sincerely for being your friend. Or appreciate your child for coming home on time.

This skill is so natural in the beginning stages of a relationship. Young lovers can't help themselves from sharing their appreciations. Mastery, however, shows up in our ability to practice this skill consciously and authentically over time. The ability to empower is like the ignition switch in the engine of outrageously fulfilling relationships.

In daily living, though, many of us withhold our love. We wait to see how the other person treats us first, to determine how we'll treat them. This kind of relating, costs us our power. We give away our power to generate love when we wait for someone else to make the first move. Think about that for a moment. We give away our power to create the very thing that determines our very quality of life; love!

To reclaim your power to create love, you must risk

giving it. You must take the initiative to empower the people in your life, knowing they may not return the favor. This may take some courage on your part. It may not be easy or familiar, just rewarding.

My brother, Bill Ferguson, is a well known author and teacher in Houston, Texas. (See www.MasteryofLife. com). Once he led an exercise on empowerment. Afterwards, when everyone else was seated, one couple remained standing. Embracing. Tears running down their cheeks. Later, he discovered that they were brother and sister, and they hadn't hugged in 37 years. And here's the clincher: They worked side by side in the family business, waiting for the other person to make the first move, just waiting. For 37 years.

Why not give yourself a special gift? Empower the people in your life while you can. You see, love is a funny thing. The more you give, the more you get. The more you give, the more you live.

FEAR OF COMMITMENT

WARNING! The following article addresses the "C" word in graphic detail. Reader discretion advised!

Why does the notion of committing, strike such fear in our hearts? Is it laziness? Cowardice, perhaps? Or is there a more substantial reason?

One of the most powerful motivators for human behavior is the avoidance of pain. Have you ever made a commitment that ended up in a major league upset? Do the words, "I will NEVER, EVER, EVER let myself get hurt like that again!!" sound familiar? How excited were you, right after a painful relationship, to jump right back into another commitment? When pain is powerfully associated with making commitment, the "C" word becomes something to avoid at all costs.

Now we've got a dilemma, because life demands commitment. We commit when we get out of bed in the morning, and when we go to work, and when we order a meal. Every time we think of our next action, and then move forward on it, we are using the dynamic of commitment.

What really happens, is that we continue making commitments. We just make them without heart.

We withhold our passion. We withhold our power. Somewhere inside we conclude that if I'm only 60% committed (and then I fail), 40% of me won't be disappointed.

Enter, the self-fulfilling prophecy. If we hold back 40% of our power, to avoid disappointment, we're only operating at 60% of capacity. That's like trying to climb Mount Everest with pneumonia. It's set up to lose. We hold back the very power needed for success. Do you know someone close to you, who lives in this chronic state of low-level commitment? Maybe someone VERY close to you.

So...do you really want to manifest the dreams of your heart? Then commit yourself fully into your chosen path. Be willing to learn from mistakes, heal through your hurt, and go for success. Watch what happens to your level of aliveness when you don't hold back. Watch what happens when two people commit to each other without reservation.

As W. H. Murray from the Scottish Himalayan expedition shared so powerfully: "Until one is committed, there is hesitancy, the chance to draw back, always ineffectiveness. Concerning all acts of initiative and creation, there is one elementary truth, the ignorance of which kills countless ideas and splendid plans: that the moment one definitely commits oneself, then Providence moves too. All sorts of things occur to help one that would never otherwise have occurred. A whole string of events issues from the decision, raising in one's favor all manner of unforeseen incidents and meetings and material assistance, which no man could have dreamed would have come his way. I have learned a deep respect for one of Goethe's couplets: 'Whatever you can do or dream you can, begin it. Boldness has genius, power, and magic in it.'"

BLOBBO VS THE KILLER TOAD...
ENDING THE CYCLE OF CONFLICT

Have you ever wondered why that "perfect couple" split up? I mean, they were so in love!...a match made in heaven!...soulmates!

Without a working knowledge of relationship dynamics, the honeymoon usually comes to a screeching halt. Love and respect turn into fear and condemnation, and they enter into a cycle of conflict. Later, she wonders what evil spell turned her white knight into Blobbo the Repulsive. And he can't figure out who turned his fairy princess into Godzilla the Killer Toad.

We've seen it in our own lives. Innocent comments escalate into World War III. Being with our partner is as much fun as digging up land mines. And almost as painful. The experience of love, which initially drew us together, is totally destroyed. A few years of torture, and it's time for Divorce Court. Or worse, we stay miserable together, until the kids are grown (like that's really doing them a favor).

This may sound like a bizarre question, but what if there's another alternative? What if there's something we can do that would end the cycle of conflict, something that could restore the peace?

There is. You have the power to heal any painful relationship. You may not have the power to change another person, but you have the power to change how you relate to that person. Here's how:

- Refuse to play the put-down game. Quit attacking. Quit taking revenge. It takes two to play tennis, only one to stop.

- Take your attention off the other person, and focus on the one person you have some control over, yourself. Look to see what you might be doing that keeps the relationship stuck. Consider this; anytime a relationship isn't working for you, it's because you are resisting some quality in that person. You are sending the message, "You are not OK the way you are." The other person gets this message from you, loud and clear, then they begin resisting you right back. The more you resist them, the more they resist you. You enter into a cycle of conflict.

- To end the cycle of conflict, give up your demand that they change. Aren't they exactly the way they are, whether you like it or not? Has your resisting them done any good? Give them permission to be the way they are. You don't necessarily have to stay with them. And you don't have to give up your personal boundaries; you can still say "no" when you need to.

There is beauty in every human being, even Blobbo and Killer Toad. You may have to search to find it, but it's there. What destroys intimacy is judgment. What creates intimacy is unconditional acceptance and deep appreciation. See the beauty in your partner, then tell them...authentically, from your heart. Over time, you might just restore mutual respect in the relationship.

For some people, these ideas represent an entirely different way of relating. Different, yes... impossible, no! In the words of Henry David Thoreau, "If you have built castles in the air, your work need not be lost; that is where they should be. Now put the foundations under them."

LISTENING FROM THE HEART

Once upon a time there was a little boy, kidnapped by bandits when he was very young. Years later, he escaped, intent on finding the village of his birth. His only memory of home, however, was the sound of his mother's voice... singing his favorite lullaby. So he traveled from village to village listening, until one day he came upon that beautiful sound. And he knew, once again, he was home.

I believe that each one of us has a mechanism in our heart that knows when a truth is spoken. It just feels right. It rings true. We also know when something doesn't sound quite right. It feels funny. There's something inside us that says, "I don't think so."

As a teacher, I try to speak to that something in each of us that resonates with the truth, that something that already knows the right choices to make. I do my best to bring out the natural wisdom already residing in people.

It wasn't always this way. My initial counseling efforts were based on a simple assumption; I know, and you don't. I couldn't figure out why clients were so resistant to following my brilliant advice. I mean, how many times did I have to tell them before they'd get the point?

Then came the big discovery; it was Randy who needed to get the point. I discovered that most people don't like to be told what to do, even if they ask. I found meaning in Carl Rogers' statement, "I couldn't presume to give you advice." I realized that people don't come to me to be advised. They come for authentic, caring support so they can make their own decisions and discover their own strengths.

From this simple insight, I discovered the most important communication tool of my life: Listening from the Heart. You could also call it non-judgmental listening or listening with compassion. When I tried this technique, it blew my socks off. My friends began opening up to me. People began to reveal and initiate their own solutions.

Listening used to mean that brief interlude when I let someone else talk. Usually, just long enough for me to think of something really important to say. Two sets of lips, flapping in the breeze. No experience of communication.

Listening from the Heart is a whole different ball game. It requires that I temporarily release my grip on the illusion that I know what's best for another. It requires that I lay aside my busy schedule, and for the moment, be truly present for someone. It requires that I give the gift of unconditional acceptance and deep appreciation. And in my silence, that I listen from a place of honoring the incredible human spirit that lives in each one of us.

Have you ever been listened to in this way? How did it feel to be in the presence of someone who loved you so much, that they would totally receive you in this way? Through their heart-centered listening, might you discover and pursue your own solutions?

What difference will it make in your special relationships when you listen from the heart?

TELLING THE MICROSCOPIC TRUTH

"Well, I couldn't tell her THAT!!"

"If he ever found out, he'd KILL me!!"

What do these statements have in common? They're representative responses to a radical challenge in relationships; telling the ABSOLUTE truth. Over the years, I've discovered that most couples harbor secrets from their partner. Big secrets. Little secrets. Secret thoughts. Secret feelings. Secret desires. Secret actions.

Do I hear a voice proclaiming, "But Randy, it's NORMAL to have secrets!?" Perhaps this is true. But I've noticed one sure way to bottom-out in the relationship department, is to follow the norm. Statistics reveal a staggering divorce rate in the U.S. What statistics don't reveal, are the number of couples who are divorced in their hearts, but continue co-habitating. Perhaps it's time to forego this lemming consciousness, and focus our attention on what works.

What works is restoring the love. Isn't it the experience of love that draws one person to another?

Two people share an unconditional acceptance and appreciation for each other. This is how relationships begin. Then, in order to avoid the risk of losing that love, we begin withholding communications. We withhold the very information that needs to be discussed, in order for the relationship to grow.

When we hold back anger and hurt, these feelings can't come forward to be healed. When we withhold expressing our boundaries, we resent ourselves for what we didn't communicate. When we withhold our past perpetrations, we nurture guilt and resentment. And often we withhold the very information a partner needs to please us. In the end, our misguided efforts to protect love, can be instrumental in its destruction.

Withholding is like climbing a mountain with a large empty sack. Every few feet, you bend down, pick up a rock, and toss it in your sack. The sack grows heavier and heavier. Soon, the adventure is no longer any fun. You forget why you wanted to climb the mountain in the first place.

I'm not suggesting you run up to your spouse saying, "Oh by the way, I had an affair with your best friend, and I don't like the way your ears stick out." You don't have to empty your sack of rocks on somebody's head.

I am suggesting a significant change in how we relate to the people we care about, to come clean in our relationships in a sensitive, co-committed manner.

The question is, "How do we create an environment of communication that literally allows anything to be discussed?" Drs. Gay and Kathlyn Hendricks have written an excellent book entitled, "Conscious Loving...the Journey to Co-commitment." Drawing from years of private practice, they outline step by step methods that can restore authentic intimacy. I recommend it.

Here are a few keys to consider:

• Begin with a stated mutual commitment to create a more meaningful level of relating, a commitment to tell the microscopic truth. Set up your ground rules for responsible and thorough conversation.

• Take turns sharing every feeling, thought, desire, judgment, and action you've been withholding especially the hard ones.

• Take full responsibility and ownership for your own feelings without blaming your partner. Give up the notion that they make you feel a certain way.

• As the emotions come up, be willing to experience them fully.

• Take full responsibility for your mistakes with a willingness to make amends.

• Commit to forgiveness.

- Restore the closeness, then keep the slate clean by communicating the microscopic truth.

When the truth is told in relationships, trust becomes a cornerstone upon which the structure of growing together, is centered.

MOM, DAD, JUST STOP IT!.. WHEN TO CONFRONT YOUR PARENTS

Have you ever noticed, our parents have magical powers? They have an uncanny ability to ruin a perfectly good day in about three words. I've seen mature, highly educated men and women brought to their emotional knees after a 5 minute chat with Mom or Dad. How do they DO that?

Does there ever come a time to confront our parents? To enforce our personal boundaries? To let them know that their words hurt? To tell them to stop it? On the other hand, is there truth in what they say? Maybe they're right. I mean, after all, they are our parents. And why does the prospect of standing up for ourselves seem so frightening?

Let's see if we can make some sense of this. To a little child, parents are like gods. All-powerful. All-knowing. And all-present. If God says, "You'll never amount to anything," or "How can you be so stupid?"...little children take these words as the gospel truth. At the same time, children know that their very survival depends upon these gods.

As these same children grow into adulthood, they may discover that Mom and Dad were wrong. They can "amount to something" and that they aren't so stupid after all. That is, until they pick up that time machine, cleverly disguised as a telephone. Then, in moments, they are 6 years old again, taking verbal arrows to the heart, while needing Mom and Dad to survive.

Ironically, the more we grow in self-esteem, the less tolerant we become of chronic verbal abuse. At some point we come to a precipice that demands we leap, that we reclaim our personal dignity.

One hot humid Texas summer, I took this leap. Dad had been sending verbal jabs my way for most of our family reunion. They were the same nagging messages he'd been telling me for years. "When are you going to grow up?" "What's the matter with you?" "When are you going to get a REAL job?"

My traditional way of coping was to acquiesce, to grin and bear it. But because I had been consciously working on myself, this time, running was not an option.

I knew I had to say something. But the very thought of confronting my dad, scared the bejeebies out of me. It was in that instant that I accidentally did something right.

Heart pounding, prepared for death, I confronted my father. With tears in my eyes, I exploded. I told him I was furious. I told him that when he talks to me that way, it hurts! It separates us! And I told him to stop it. I told him that he matters to me. I told him I wanted to be close to him and that I loved him with all my heart.

Dad sat there in a state of shock. I'd never spoken like this to him. Not ever. Then this gruff, unfeeling monster stood up. He took me in his arms. And wept.

He said that he had no idea that he was hurting me so. He said he was sorry, that he just didn't know. Then he told me that he loved me. Our relationship was never the same after that. The love and respect we shared until his final days was priceless.

There were a couple major gifts of learning in this event for me. First of all, there is a time to stand up for what I truly believe is right. Secondly, I learned that there is a difference between attacking and confronting. Attacking is about blaming; it provokes defensiveness and retaliation. Confronting comes from a commitment to make things better and strongly communicates one's profound caring for another.

So what does this have to do with outrageously fulfilling relationships? A lot! Unless we know when and how to stand up for ourselves, we become dependent on others for our self esteem. This dependence is a road map to disaster in relationships.

One more suggestion here. You might want to get

some support from a qualified independent third party, like a really good counselor. (I emphasize 'good' because there are both good and lousy counselors. Do your research.) The insight, straight talk and encouragement you receive can help you to deliver your communications with compassion and discernment. Hey, why not stack the odds in your favor?

WHY THE GRASS IS ALWAYS GREENER
ON MY SIDE OF THE FENCE

There's a story of an Ethiopian woman who could only watch as her two small children starved to death. First one and then the other, cradled in her arms.

A short while later, she was befriended by a missionary who took her on as a traveling assistant. On her first visit to the United States, she was asked to pick up some groceries at the local supermarket. There, in the produce department, she saw polished apples in meticulous display; oranges, bananas, grapes, carrots and potatoes. Full and flawless, under spotlights with music in the background.

She was trying not to cry, when a young floor sweeper saw the tears in her eyes. Gently, he asked her if he could be of assistance. To which she replied, "No, thank you. I was just thinking, if only a short while ago, I had the pieces of fruit in front of your broom, my children might be alive today."

When I heard this story, it touched something very deep in me. I noticed two things about the way I live my life:

1) No matter how wonderful things are, I can find something to complain about; and 2) I really have it very, very, very good.

This gentle woman, who would have treasured a bit of garbage to feed her little ones, inspires me to take notice of how I perceive my surroundings. Do I focus on my lack, or do I focus on the gifts surrounding me? The answer seems important, because we know that whatever we focus upon, expands.

The more I focus on (and appreciate) what I have, the richer I feel inside. The more I focus on what's missing, the more I feel an emptiness in my heart, and no amount of accumulating seems to satisfy my need.

Isn't this particularly true in relationships? After being alone for some time, I might especially appreciate a new partner. I might look forward to being with her and treasure her company. However, let a little time pass, and my appreciation gives way to judgment and expectation. Soon, I'm taking her for granted, feeling trapped, thinking the grass might be greener elsewhere.

What I've discovered is that it doesn't have to be this way; I have a choice in the matter. I can consciously choose to appreciate.

If you have been feeling a little on the empty side, this simple exercise might make a difference:

- Make a list of people who are closest to you. Next to each person's name, write down what you really appreciate about them.

- Then take the time to thank them, from your heart.

- Notice that the feeling of prosperity isn't created by obtaining more. The feeling of prosperity is created by appreciating what you already have. To create prosperity in relationships, consciously appreciate the people who are already in your life. The greater your gratitude, the greater your wealth.

Then you can turn to someone and say, "You know what? The grass is always greener on MY side of the fence."

RESTORING LOVE IN YOUR FAMILY

Unless your parents happened to be named Ozzie and Harriet, you may have been raised in a family that was less than perfect. Some of you may have been raised in a family steeped in verbal and/or physical abuse. In your own way, you may have tried to restore the intimacy...but without tools and support, you may have eventually given up hope. To be in their presence may have become so painful, you may have decided to create as much distance as possible.

This strategy is not bad...it has served a purpose. Yet, as you evolve as a person, you may come to a point where old methods of relating, no longer serve you. You may notice that no matter how many miles separate you from your family, they still live somewhere deep in your heart. Although you may not think of them often, when you do, there is a pang of hurting. This is because no matter how atrocious your history, the love from one family member to another, cannot be destroyed. It can be buried...but not destroyed.

Often, people don't take the initiative to heal family relationships until threatened with losing someone they used to care about. After decades of distance, they come to the hospital and make their peace. At the funeral, the real sadness is about years of intimacy lost, for not having cleared emotional differences. If you have an interest in restoring closeness in your family, there may be something you can do.

Steps to Restoring Love in the Family:

Step 1) Recognize that whenever you resent, where that resentment lives, is in your own heart. Resentment costs you your peace, your health, and perhaps your family. So begin the healing process for your own benefit.

Step 2) Create the willingness to forgive them. If you are unwilling to forgive...that's OK. However there is a consequence; you get to keep the resentment and all the consequences that go with it. Remember, forgiveness doesn't mean you approve of what they did. Forgiveness is about creating peace inside of you.

Step 3) Recognize they did the best they could with a very limited reality. If they were wiser and more aware, they would have done things differently...but they weren't. They messed up...just like you have in your own way. Forgive them from the bottom of your heart, then forgive yourself...because you, too, did the best you could with limited wisdom.

Step 4) Often feelings of sadness and compassion surface when you move into forgiveness. Allow these feelings. They are a natural part of the healing process.

Step 5) After you have healed the resentment inside yourself, you may want to contact members of your family. Let them know they matter to you...that you want to heal the relationship now, instead of later. Give them permission to react however they do, and stand firm in your caring.

Be patient. This process may take some time, and a good counselor can be priceless in the process.

This journey is not for the weak of heart. And it most likely will bring up every issue from the past you can imagine. Yet, when love is restored in family relationships, there's a separateness that falls away. There's a knowing for the people we hold dear, that we have always loved one another on the deepest level. And the more we heal our past, the less baggage we bring into our romantic relationships.

One of the best books I've ever read on creating an outrageously wonderful family environment is Steven Vannoy's book, The 10 Greatest Gifts I Give My Children. I definitely put this one in the "must read" department.

When you look back on your own life some day, what will it feel like to know in your heart, that you made a powerful positive impact on the people you've loved the most?

OVERCOMING JEALOUSY

You're out for dinner. Your special someone runs into an old friend, a very attractive member of the opposite sex. They're smiling...flirting, in fact. You're sure of it!

That old familiar anger starts to surge in the pit of your stomach. Your mind races to drastic measures: Leave the party. Slam the door. Punch somebody's lights out.

What's it like to experience jealousy? Sure, there's the thrill of fine drama with its surge of adrenaline, but ultimately jealousy becomes very expensive. It costs you your peace, your joy, your dignity, and often the relationship itself.

Overcoming jealousy may seem an impossible mission...kind of like teaching Frankenstein to sit, shake, and roll over. But it can be done if you're fed up enough. Here's a beginning:

Step 1) Notice that you're jealous. Once you admit it, you can begin to deal with it. Denial keeps you stuck, and really isn't that attractive.

Step 2) Take your focus off the other person, and notice what's going on with you. You're the one that's going crazy. The other person is just doing whatever they do...and you're in a world of upset. Notice that you have very limited control over another person's actions. Focus your attention on the one person who can really do something.

Step 3) Release your attachment. Attachment is not love. Attachment destroys love. It's that clinging to another that stifles relationships. When you're attached to someone, you drive them away. Let them go...in your heart. Give them permission to be gone from your life, forever.

Step 4) When you truly experience letting someone go, you may notice a sadness come up. Perhaps it's coming up to be healed. In the privacy of a safe place, create a willingness to feel all that hurt. Don't fight the hurt. Let it come. Cry, if you can. It's hurt from the present, and hurt from the past. Let it come and let it go. Embrace yourself in your hurting, just as you would a small child. Love yourself through this process until you've cried the last tear.

Step 5) At this point you may feel a peace...a knowing that you will be fine, regardless of another's actions. This is true freedom. From this place of clarity you can make effective decisions. You may discover that there really was nothing to be concerned about. Or, if your partner has a pattern of cheating, you may choose to end a dysfunctional relationship. You may also elect to address the issue head on with an effective counselor.

Then congratulate yourself for caring enough to take courageous action. Remember, for the rest of your life, you will always have a relationship with yourself, and no one can ever take that away.

SELF FORGIVENESS

Have you ever blown it...really big? I mean really, REALLY big? Have you ever made huge mistakes where you've hurt the people you love the most? I just did. And it's not the first time.

My inner conversation sounds like this:

Randy: "How could you have been such an idiot? You should have known better. Why didn't you think ahead? What's the matter with you?"

I feel ashamed. I feel like my heart's been replaced with a ten pound shot put. And I want to find a big rock to go crawl under.

Do you know this feeling?

As painful as this moment is right now, I see that I have some very important choices to make. Am I going into that downward spiral of self-condemnation, or am I going to move into a mode of healing? Will I create more damage, or am I going to do what works?

To choose what works, is to choose self-forgiveness, learning, and making amends. And this is true whether or not I feel like I deserve it. Herein lies the opportunity for a little self counseling.

A first step in self-forgiveness is to move out of the denial, and into the truth...to let go of my justification, my blaming others, and my self-condemnation. So here is a dialogue that might help:

Self Counselor: Did you really do what you did?.. and...did your actions really have the consequences that they had?

Randy: Very clearly, the answer is "yes," on both counts.

Self Counselor: A second step is to recognize that you are on a path of learning. You learn by participating in life. The more you go for it, the more mistakes you make. The more mistakes you make, the more you learn. So blowing it, is actually a vital ingredient to growing in your wisdom. The question is, are you willing to make mistakes, since that's the way life works?

Randy: Yes, I am. I don't like it, but I'm willing.

Self Counselor: A third step is to give up demanding the impossible. Whenever you make the statement, "I should have known better," you are saying that you should have had the wisdom from your lesson before you learned it. In the school of life, first you get the test, then you get the lesson. Are you willing to forgive yourself for not knowing in advance?

Randy: Yes. I see that there's no way I could have had the wisdom before I learned the lesson.

Self Counselor: So are you willing to forgive yourself since you couldn't have known to handle things differently? Are you willing to forgive yourself for being fallible, for being human?

Randy: Yes, I am. I see that I'm just a human being. No more, no less. I see that the longer I go without self-forgiveness, the more my self-esteem is damaged. And the lower my self esteem, the less capable I am in relationships and life.

The truth is, I wouldn't hurt if I didn't care, and it is in my caring that my preciousness lives...even when I blow it really, really big.

CREATING ECSTASY...
NOW, NOT SOMEDAY

Imagine. Right there in your hand. The winning Lotto ticket! More money than you know how to spend. How do you feel? Ecstatic? Totally charged? Invincible? Outrageous?

So what do you want first, the good news or the bad news? OK, I'll give you the bad news. The bad news is you do not really have the winning lotto ticket, and you are far more likely to get struck by lightning (while dancing the Tango in your pajamas) than to ever win the big one.

The good news is that you do not have to win the lotto to feel ecstatic, totally charged, invincible, and outrageous.

Consider this. In our culture, we have been taught that happiness comes from doingness and havingness. As soon as I find the right partner, as soon as I land that big job, as soon as I lose twenty pounds, as soon as I win the lottery, as soon as I (fill in the blank), THEN I will feel ecstatic, totally charged, invincible, and outrageous. THEN, I will finally have love in my life. In other words, we try to "do" and "have' to get to love.

Do you see the con game here? We have this laundry list of self-imposed requirements to be fulfilled before we can really enjoy life. What goes unnoticed, is that the list grows faster than our ability to check the items off. The result is, we live in a perpetual state of being not OK. I call it, "Living in the Land of Someday."

There is a better way. If you speak to one of those fortunate few who cherish their outrageously fulfilling relationships, they may let you in on a little secret; that happiness does not come from doingness or even havingness. And it especially does not come from their partner.

It works the other way around. People who are truly effective, first create happiness, then take action. From the peace they create in their heart, they have the clarity to move forward. First they "love" then they "do"...then they "have." They bring their outrageous fulfillment TO the relationship.

"But Randy, you don't know all the hassles I'm dealing with. There is no way I can just be happy!"

I hear you. However, please know, it is not the circumstances in our lives that make us unhappy. If you can afford to buy this book, there are literally billions of people who would be thrilled to have your problems. What makes us unhappy is our resistance to the circumstances. The more we resist the way life is, the more we suffer. The more we accept and appreciate the way our life is, the more we prosper. And whether we resist or accept, is a choice we each get to make from moment to moment.

Who you are, right now, is a precious human being. You do not have to win the Lotto or have a beautiful partner to feel ecstatic, totally charged, invincible, and outrageous. Dan Millman puts it well. He says simply, "There are no ordinary moments." The time to cherish your life is now, but only if you say so.

GOLD AT YOUR FEET...
RENEWING RELATIONSHIPS

The old miner spent his life searching for the gold he knew would make him a happy man. One day, his pick finally struck into that precious yellow metal. In ecstasy, he gathered every last tiny nugget, until his pouch was full. It was only after his long hike to town that he remembered a small hole, he'd been meaning to mend. Desperately, he pulled out his pouch, just in time to watch the last glimmering flake as it fell to his feet.

It seems to me that many couples who have been together for some time, are very much like this old miner. Falling in love is like finally discovering buried treasure. At last, I've found the acceptance and appreciation I've been searching for! Life now, is about living happily ever after.

But time passes. The pounding in my heart, when she enters the room, gives way to more pressing concerns. Did you pick up my laundry today? You spent how much for junior's new shoes!? I thought YOU let the puppies out.

At some point we begin to notice, the love that drew us together has slowly been leaking out of our pouch.

And many of us don't discover the leak until our hearts are empty.

It doesn't have to be this way. If only you are willing, the leak can be mended, and the pouch refilled. Here are some keys you might want to consider:

Recognize that love is, among other things, a resource. The presence or absence of loving, is what makes or breaks relationships. In fact, it's what makes or breaks our very quality of life. Love is your very life force, far more precious than gold.

Often we wait for the other person to make the first move toward reconciliation. This is usually a mistake. The moment I say it's up to another to restore love in a relationship, I give away my power to create love to someone else.

At any given moment, we are either creating love or destroying it. The experience of love is created by consciously and authentically giving the gift of unconditional acceptance and deep appreciation. We leak love through our condemnation and taking for granted. What it takes to have love, is to give love.

If your relationship is running on empty, you might consider the following experiment. Think of ten things your partner would really love to receive from you. Kind words, flowers, a back rub, a favorite meal, etc. Then give it, unconditionally. Don't tell them what you're up to. Just do it, over time. (For details read Harville Hendrix' fabulous book, "Getting the Love You Want").

A while back, I tried this with the most difficult person I've ever had to deal with, my ex-wife. Shortly after, she called me. She didn't want anything from me. She just wanted to check in to see how I was doing, and to tell me she loves me.

OUTRAGEOUSNESS...
A SIGN OF MASTERY
IN RELATIONSHIPS

On a frigid first day of January, I became an official member of the Colorado Polar Bear Club.

Membership is simple. Pay a small fee...walk barefoot through the snow to a hole carved in ice...and back flip into the Boulder Reservoir.

You ask, "Why on earth would any mature adult do anything that stupid?" And what does this have to do with relationships? I answer, "Read on. There is a method to my madness."

Imagine a box which we'll label as your "comfort zone." Now imagine yourself living day to day within the confines of this box. Outside this box, live your dreams, what you really would love to have, and who you really would love to be.

One day you decide to go for your dreams. You leave your place of comfort, and begin taking the action required to make your dreams reality. Then you notice that in approaching your dreams, things begin to get a little scary..a little uncomfortable. Behold the comfort zone!

Your mind offers every reason to quit. To move forward seems crazy...unreasonable...outrageous. I mean, what would people think?

At this point, many folks usually make a U-turn and high-tail it back to the land of comfort. They return to the center of the box. And there they stay; comfortable, and more than a little disgusted with themselves. Then they go home and blame their spouse for their own self-inflicted frustration. And their dreams? Their dreams live forever in the realm of "someday."

What would happen, however, if you never made that U-turn?...if you blasted through that box, on toward your dreams? Can you recall a time in your life when you pressed through the comfort zone, and accomplished the very thing you thought you couldn't? What did that feel like? Didn't you experience a vibrant aliveness? Do you remember that surge of energy when you got bigger than your fear? And in that moment of victory, how did you feel about the people around you?

Please consider this. One of the greatest gifts you can give yourself (and your relationships) is to live your life outrageously. To earnestly and tenaciously go for your dreams. For some inspiring reading on this topic, pick up the book, Do It!. Let's Get Off Our Buts by John Roger and Peter McWilliams.

As for my dip on New Year's Day, perhaps it was a little crazy. It certainly was uncomfortable. But as I recall the laughter and exhilaration of my fellow

Polar Bears, I see very clearly how I want to live my life.

DISCOVERING A RELATIONSHIP WITH SPIRIT

The very topic of spirituality is a touchy one. It is an arena that is intensely personal for most people and certainly a source of highly diverse and strongly held opinions. Accordingly, I preface this writing with the admission that I do not consider myself wise enough to tell anyone what they should believe. In the same breath, however, I am compelled to share a spiritual perspective that has made a profound difference in the quality of my own life.

With great love and respect, I share some insights that have worked for me. Please accept those that resonate in your heart, and disregard the rest.

When I first began leading seminars, I was amazed to discover how many people harbored negative feelings on the topic of spirituality. They shared an array of experiences that I could only categorize as religious abuse. To them, God meant guilt, fear, shame and hypocrisy. I could certainly understand why they felt the way they did. Yet, I also saw in them a yearning to connect with some loving higher power; a different kind of God.

If perhaps I am describing your spiritual history, allow me to suggest a new possibility. Perhaps the people who hit you over the head with religious tyranny are not the final authorities on the subject. Perhaps you ran from their teachings with good reason. Yet, in your efforts to escape a dysfunctional environment, you may have thrown the "spiritual baby" out with the bath water. If so, there may be an enormously valuable gift available to you. Consider the possibility of a spiritual life based upon honoring the precious essence you truly are, and respecting your learning process.

For me, there is incredible joy and fulfillment in my spiritual life. There is a peace, a sense of being cared for and guided, regardless of how life looks in any particular moment. In following my spiritual guidance, I am able to live in alignment with my own inner values, free of guilt.

When I blow it, as I so often do, there is forgiveness and getting back on track. In the experience of true forgiveness, self-judgment falls away, replaced with deep self-loving. Ironically, the greater my surrender to this unseen presence, the greater is my experience of freedom.

When two or more people come into partnership with Spirit, they begin sharing these gifts together. When times get tough between them, they have a spiritual common ground they can access. They experience being in partnership with an all-power-ful, all-present, all-knowing, all-loving source. Not a bad partner to have, if you think about it.

To create a relationship with Spirit, you must ask for a relationship with Spirit. Ask with all your heart. You may discover that what opens the door to your spirituality is your ability to love, to give the gift of unconditional acceptance and deep appreciation. What closes the door is your judgment and harsh condemnation. Whether this door remains open or closed is a choice we all get to make from moment to moment.

May we choose well.

THE GATEWAY

Just for a moment, recall a time when you were in the experience of love. Recall a time when you were in the presence of someone who truly loved you... with all their heart. Notice what that feels like inside. If you can read this book immersed in that memory, you may discover a way to access something you've been looking for.

Look in your heart, and you will discover that the experience of love is so much more than mere emotion. Love is a gateway. The instant we create the experience of love, regardless of our current life circumstance, we pass through a magical opening. We enter a dimension where life works brilliantly.

Look in your heart, and you will discover that peace is love at rest, and joy is love at play. There is no peace or joy without the experience of love.

Look in your heart, and you will discover that love and fear are mutually exclusive. In the state of love, a sense of safety presides...a knowing you'll be fine, regardless of what happens.

Look in your heart, and you will discover love generates the deep satisfaction of being in the moment. Stress and the urgency to achieve, are replaced with a delight in being who you are...where you are...with what you have..and who you're with.

Look in your heart, and you will discover that the experience of love brings forth the qualities of a child... an authentic vulnerabi1ity...a sweetness...a playful spontaneity...a presence you want to wrap your arms around.

Look in your heart, and you will discover that healing is the application of loving to hurt. Emotions are greeted with compassion...allowed to be expressed and completed. Physical hurting is regarded as the body's cry for attention...a cry that is heeded. And in the instant of love fully experienced, there is no suffering.

Look in your heart, and you will discover in the validation love provides, that creativity taps into a higher source...and generates energy beyond measure.

Look in your heart, and you will discover that love is the source of all just law. It does not conform to the harsh mandates of man...but holds steadfast, in the face of ignorance and confusion.

Look in your heart, and you will discover that creating the experience of love is paramount in any working relationship with another...with yourself...with life...and with Spirit. Maybe this is why Emmet Fox has described love as "the golden gate of paradise." It seems to me that, at any given moment, we are on one side of this gate, or the other. We are either creating the experience of love or destroying it. What it takes to create the experience of love, is to give love. To consciously give the gift of unconditional acceptance and deep appreciation.

Perhaps, if we look deeply enough into our hearts, we will discover that who we are is so much more than a name, a body, a title or a collection of assets. Perhaps we'll discover that we are more an experience than we are a thing. Just maybe, we'll discover that who we are IS love. And that to live life on the love side of the gate, is to live congruently with who we are; sacred human beings, invited to create and treasure outrageously fulfilling relationships.

A Possibility for You...
An Enormous Leap in Personal Effectiveness

For years I've been engaged in the question, "What does it take to generate and sustain a massive, positive and sustainable shift in people's lives?" From this exploration, the Love, Courage and Achievement Project was born.

The LCA begins with a no-cost person to person interview to determine whether this work is a fit for each participant...or not. Only those with a particularly strong commitment to their own personal development are accepted into the program. Just imagine the energy in a room full of folks who are really serious about transforming their lives! (Could that be you?)

The next step is the LCA Weekend Retreat, which is held in the Denver, Colorado area. In this three-day event, people release the mental/emotional baggage that has held them back...not just intellectually, but in their hearts. Through experiential exercises, a host of new tools, and the support from one another...they cry, they laugh, and they reclaim their ability to live in the experience of love.

After the LCA Weekend Retreat, guess what? People are immersed right back into the families and culture that taught them so much of what doesn't work in the first place! So what's needed at this point, is an effective means of integration and sustainability. That is the purpose of the LCA 6-Week Course.

For 6 evenings, once a week, we explore key areas that are essential for living an outrageously fulfilling life. Topics include: Regaining Your Personal Power, Healing Upsets, Mastery in Relationships, Creating Outrageous Prosperity, Discovering and Manifesting Life Purpose, and Practicing Celebration as a Resource.

Other aspects of the LCA 6-Week Course include the small Champion Teams, a Buddy System, a powerful set of breakthrough tools, the LCA Workbook, Bill Ferguson's Mastery of Life CD album and book, Miracles Are Guaranteed. Individual coaching sessions and ongoing discussion groups are also part of this support system.

Of course we make life-long friends in the process. Other benefit-biggies include supercharging your quality of life, reclaiming your joy and of course, manifesting outrageously fulfilling relationships.

So what's next? There are two key questions we ask people to consider before participating in the initial interview:

Question #1) What are the unworkabilites in your life?

As the word would imply, an unworkability is any area of your life that is currently not working as well as you would like. Internal unworkabilities include fear, destructive anger, past hurt, guilt, resentment, toxic stress, self judgment, etc. External unworkabilities include romantic and family relationships, career, finances, health, living environment, etc. Basically, what we are looking for is a list of any areas of your life where you would like to see a constructive change.

Question #2) What are the dreams of your heart?

What are those things that if you could have them, do them or be them...it would bring great joy to your heart?

When you have completed your lists, you are invited to call us to set up a no-cost interview where together, we can determine whether or not this work is appropriate for you.

Also, please feel free to explore our website:

www.LCAProject.com

IN CLOSING

You might consider the ideas presented in this book to be pieces of a magical puzzle. Listen to your heart, and arrange the pieces as you will. Add to them. Subtract from them. Enjoy learning what works, and what doesn't. Create with them a unique and evolving picture for your Self and your relationships. Discover what fulfills your sense of duty, what resonates with Spirit, what gives you joy and what you know to be true.

Here is a challenge for us all. Let's not play small. Remember the thoughts you had, about your having something oh-so-special to offer to world? Well, you do! Let your passion to make a difference, grow bigger than any fear of rejection. Step into being who you have always known you were meant to be. Accept God's gift and give us your masterpiece.

And if, in the process, you choose to share your journey with a lifemate, base your relationship on the principles of love. So in parting for now, I leave you with a profound question to consider "Just how good are you willing to have it?" With love and respect, Randy Ferguson.

Bibliography

Ferguson, Bill. *Have You Suffered Enough?* Return to the Heart. Houston, Texas. 2002.

Ferguson, Bill. *How to Heal a Painful Relationship, And If Necessary, Part As Friends.* Return to the Heart. Houston, Texas. 1999.

Ferguson, Bill. *Mastery of Life* Audio Course. Return to the Heart. Houston, Texas. 2003.

Ferguson,Bill. *Miracles Are Guaranteed.* Return to the Heart. Houston, Texas. 1992.

Hendricks, Gay and Kathlyn. *Conscious Loving, the Journey to Co-commitment.* Bantam. New York, New York. 1990.

Hendrix, Harville. *Getting the Love You Want, A Guide for Couples.* Harper Perennial. New York, New York. 1988

John-Roger and McWilliams, Peter. *Do It, Let's Get Off Our Buts.* Prelude Press. Los Angeles, California, 1991.

Vannoy, Steven. *The 10 Greatest Gifts I Give My Children.* Simon and Schuster. New York, New York. 1994.

ABOUT THE AUTHOR..

I love sharing nuggets of insight and asking questions that pull forward the wisdom that already lives in my readers and seminar participants. Why? Because I firmly believe that raising the level of people's wisdom is the most effective way of creating positive sustainable change on our planet. Just like you, the opportunity to make a constructive difference in someone's life, provides a never-ending source of motivation for me.

My first personal development seminars began in 1978. Since then, I have been blessed with meeting thousands of participants, each a teacher in his or her own right, from whom I have grown tremendously.

Through Pathways to Leadership, a corporate culture-building program, I've been privileged to teach breakthrough leadership skills in the U.S, Mexico, Thailand, Germany and Spain. Our clients have included Ford, United Airlines, Mazda, Caraustar, International Truck and Engine, Schering Plough and the U.S Government.

OK. You want to know my official credentials. I have two: 1) A Masters degree in Spiritual Psychology from the University of Santa Monica (an outrageously fulfilling university if there ever was one); and 2) the knowing that even a fool can say a wise thing.

Gail and I are planning to marry, and a beautiful precocious seven year old daughter comes with the deal. Am I a lucky guy or what?! And can you guess our common purpose? It's to create an outrageously fulfilling family, of course! Until then, I live in Denver, Colorado with my pet fish.

Newspaper and Magazine Publishers:

If you have an interest in publishing these brief chapters in your periodical, please contact us.

The Love, Courage and Achievement Project
Attention: Randy Ferguson
7101 W Yale Ave #3603
Denver, CO 80227
Phone: 303-989-2605

www.LCAProject.com

To Order More Copies

Call 303-989-2605 to place your orders over the phone. (And yes!!... you actually get to speak to a real person!) Order on line at: **www.LCAProject.com** or complete this form and mail in.

	Price	Qty.	Amount
Outrageously Fulfilling Relationships (Paperback)	$13.95	____	_____
Outrageously Fulfilling Relationships (Book on CD)	$21.95	____	_____
Subtotal			_____
Colorado Residents add 8% sales tax			_____
Shipping and Handling			$4.50
Plus 10% of subtotal			_____
Total			_____

Name (Please print): _____

Address: _____

City: _____ State: _____ Zip: Code: _____

Telephone: Day - _____ Eve. - _____

E-Mail Address: _____

Please make checks or money orders payable to:
Heart Centered Communications, Inc.   and send to 7101 W Yale Ave #3603, Denver, CO 80227

For Credit Card Orders:

Card No.: _____

Total $: _____   Expiration Date: _____

Signature: _____

Notes:

Notes:

Notes:

Notes:

Notes: